HELPFUL PEOPLE

CHEF

JAMIE FICKETT

Norwood House Press

Library of Congress Cataloging-in-Publication Data:

Names: Fickett, Jamie.
Title: Chef / Jamie Fickett.
Description: Buffalo, NY : Norwood House Press, 2025. | Series: Helpful people | Includes glossary and index.
Identifiers: ISBN 9781684503100 (pbk.) | ISBN 9781684503117 (library bound) | ISBN 9781684503124 (ebook
Subjects: LCSH: Cooks--Juvenile literature.
Classification: LCC TX652.5 F535 2025 | DDC 641.5--dc23

Published in 2025 by
Norwood House Press
2544 Clinton Street
Buffalo, NY 14224

Designer: Ocean Books
Editor: Kim Thompson

Photo credits: Cover, p. 1 bbernard/Shutterstock.com; p. 5 Jacob Lund/Shutterstock.com; p. 6 lunamarina/Shutterstock.com; p. 7 E[illegible] Woo/Shutterstock.com; p. 9 Candy Retriever/Shutterstock.com; p. 11 Gorodenkoff/Shutterstock.com; p. 12 Drazen Zigic/Shutterstock.com; p. 13 Lee Waranyu/Shutterstock.com; p. 15 Peter Mayer 67/ Shutterstock.com; p. 16 photoAZ/Shutterstock.com; p. 17David Tadevosian/Shutterstock.com; pp. 19, 21 wavebreakmedia/Shutterstock.com

Printed in the United States of America

Some of the images in this book illustrate individuals who are models. The depictions do not imply actual situations or events.

CPSIA compliance information: Batch #CW25NHP: For further information contact Norwood House Press at 1-800-237-9932.

Find us on

TABLE OF CONTENTS

What Is a Chef? 4
What Does a Chef Wear? 10
What Tools Does a Chef Use? 14
How Do You Become a Chef? 18
Glossary 22
Thinking Questions 23
Index 24
About the Author 24

WHAT IS A CHEF?

Chefs are important helpers in our **community**. They cook meals. They work in restaurants, schools, and hospitals to make delicious food.

Chefs create new recipes for people to try. They think about what foods taste good together. Then, they invent new dishes.

Some chefs work at big events like weddings or parties. They prepare food for lots of guests.

Chefs can help people learn about healthy foods. They choose **ingredients** that are good for our bodies.

WHAT DOES A CHEF WEAR?

Many chefs wear a **uniform**. One part of the uniform is a chef's coat. The coat protects chefs from spills and hot splashes.

Chefs also wear tall white hats called **toques**. The hat keeps their hair out of the food.

Chefs often wear an apron. The apron covers their front so their clothes do not get dirty.

Chefs wear shoes that are comfortable and that do not slip. They cover the chef's feet completely to protect them from hot spills or dropped **utensils**.

WHAT TOOLS DOES A CHEF USE?

Chefs use a lot of different **tools** to help them cook.

Knives chop vegetables, cut meat, and slice bread. They need to be sharp to cut things safely.

Chefs stir ingredients together in mixing bowls. Mixing bowls come in different sizes.

Pots and pans go on the stove and in the oven. Pots are used for boiling water or making soups. Pans are used for frying or **sautéing** food.

HOW DO YOU BECOME A CHEF?

After finishing high school, some future chefs go to **culinary** school. Culinary school is where chefs learn how to make fancy meals.

Many new chefs work under other chefs. They learn by doing real cooking in a restaurant.

Chefs are creative. They pay close attention to their cooking to make sure everything tastes just right. Good chefs care about making food that everyone will enjoy eating.